AF884858

Stock Trading Calendar

2026

Roselis Publications
Copyright (c) 2026
www.roselispublications.com

2026

January

S	M	T	W	T	F	S
				1	2	3
4	5	6	7	8	9	10
11	12	13	14	15	16	17
18	19	20	21	22	23	24
25	26	27	28	29	30	31

February

S	M	T	W	T	F	S
1	2	3	4	5	6	7
8	9	10	11	12	13	14
15	16	17	18	19	20	21
22	23	24	25	26	27	28

March

S	M	T	W	T	F	S
1	2	3	4	5	6	7
8	9	10	11	12	13	14
15	16	17	18	19	20	21
22	23	24	25	26	27	28
29	30	31				

April

S	M	T	W	T	F	S
			1	2	3	4
5	6	7	8	9	10	11
12	13	14	15	16	17	18
19	20	21	22	23	24	25
26	27	28	29	30		

May

S	M	T	W	T	F	S
					1	2
3	4	5	6	7	8	9
10	11	12	13	14	15	16
17	18	19	20	21	22	23
24	25	26	27	28	29	30
31						

June

S	M	T	W	T	F	S
	1	2	3	4	5	6
7	8	9	10	11	12	13
14	15	16	17	18	19	20
21	22	23	24	25	26	27
28	29	30				

July

S	M	T	W	T	F	S
			1	2	3	4
5	6	7	8	9	10	11
12	13	14	15	16	17	18
19	20	21	22	23	24	25
26	27	28	29	30	31	

August

S	M	T	W	T	F	S
						1
2	3	4	5	6	7	8
9	10	11	12	13	14	15
16	17	18	19	20	21	22
23	24	25	26	27	28	29
30	31					

September

S	M	T	W	T	F	S
		1	2	3	4	5
6	7	8	9	10	11	12
13	14	15	16	17	18	19
20	21	22	23	24	25	26
27	28	29	30			

October

S	M	T	W	T	F	S
				1	2	3
4	5	6	7	8	9	10
11	12	13	14	15	16	17
18	19	20	21	22	23	24
25	26	27	28	29	30	31

November

S	M	T	W	T	F	S
1	2	3	4	5	6	7
8	9	10	11	12	13	14
15	16	17	18	19	20	21
22	23	24	25	26	27	28
29	30					

December

S	M	T	W	T	F	S
		1	2	3	4	5
6	7	8	9	10	11	12
13	14	15	16	17	18	19
20	21	22	23	24	25	26
27	28	29	30	31		

Stock Trading Calendar 2026

Contents

Section 1

Calendar Key

Each monthly calendar highlights notable days that may impact trading, such as holidays and stock market closings. Other notable time periods are indicated with these symbols:

Third Fridays - Most stock options (calls and puts) expire on the third Friday of the month. Traders may close, roll over, or exercise contracts, which can increase trading volume and volatility. Price discrepancies can also arise between underlying stocks and their derivatives. These events can lead to sharp price swings near the close due to high volume and forced rebalancing.

Full Moon - The full moon is believed by some traders and researchers to have a psychological and behavioral impact on financial markets, although it's not universally accepted or proven in mainstream finance. A well-known 2003 study by Yuan, Zheng, and Zhu ("Are Investors Moonstruck?") found that stock returns tend to be lower on and around full moon days in global markets. However, given the massive complexity and many influencing factors in markets, any moon-phase effect is likely very small and unreliable.

☿ **Mercury retrograde periods,** like full moons, are cited as bad times for making big decisions or taking risks. Some traders claim the markets can become volatile, irrational, or prone to reversals during Mercury retrograde periods, which occur 3–4 times per year for about 3 weeks each. These time periods are hereby noted on the monthly calendar for those who take this into consideration. While retrograde periods may subtly affect trader behavior due to belief and media buzz, this should not replace data-driven trading strategies or fundamental/technical analysis.

Mercury Retrograde Period	Dates
First Retrograde	February 26-March 20, 2026
Second Retrograde	June 29-July 23, 2026
Third Retrograde	October 24-November 13, 2026

"The safest way to double your money is to fold it over and put it in your pocket."
– Kin Hubbard

JANUARY 2026

SUN	MON	TUE	WED	THU	FRI	SAT
				1 New Year's Day Market Closed	2	3 Wolf Moon
4	5	6	7	8	9	10
11	12	13	14	15	16	17
18	19 M L King Day Market Closed	20	21	22	23	24
25	26	27	28	29	30	31

January 2026 Trading Log Week 1

Monday

Company	Opening Price	ATR	Volume	Entry Price	Target Price	Stop Loss	Notes/Results

Tuesday

Company	Opening Price	ATR	Volume	Entry Price	Target Price	Stop Loss	Notes/Results

Wednesday

Company	Opening Price	ATR	Volume	Entry Price	Target Price	Stop Loss	Notes/Results

Thursday

Company	Opening Price	ATR	Volume	Entry Price	Target Price	Stop Loss	Notes/Results

Friday

Company	Opening Price	ATR	Volume	Entry Price	Target Price	Stop Loss	Notes/Results

January 2026 Trading Log Week 2

Monday

Company	Opening Price	ATR	Volume	Entry Price	Target Price	Stop Loss	Notes/Results

Tuesday

Company	Opening Price	ATR	Volume	Entry Price	Target Price	Stop Loss	Notes/Results

Wednesday

Company	Opening Price	ATR	Volume	Entry Price	Target Price	Stop Loss	Notes/Results

Thursday

Company	Opening Price	ATR	Volume	Entry Price	Target Price	Stop Loss	Notes/Results

Friday

Company	Opening Price	ATR	Volume	Entry Price	Target Price	Stop Loss	Notes/Results

January 2026 Trading Log Week 3

Monday

Company	Opening Price	ATR	Volume	Entry Price	Target Price	Stop Loss	Notes/Results

Tuesday

Company	Opening Price	ATR	Volume	Entry Price	Target Price	Stop Loss	Notes/Results

Wednesday

Company	Opening Price	ATR	Volume	Entry Price	Target Price	Stop Loss	Notes/Results

Thursday

Company	Opening Price	ATR	Volume	Entry Price	Target Price	Stop Loss	Notes/Results

Friday

Company	Opening Price	ATR	Volume	Entry Price	Target Price	Stop Loss	Notes/Results

January 2026 Trading Log Week 4

Monday

Company	Opening Price	ATR	Volume	Entry Price	Target Price	Stop Loss	Notes/Results

Tuesday

Company	Opening Price	ATR	Volume	Entry Price	Target Price	Stop Loss	Notes/Results

Wednesday

Company	Opening Price	ATR	Volume	Entry Price	Target Price	Stop Loss	Notes/Results

Thursday

Company	Opening Price	ATR	Volume	Entry Price	Target Price	Stop Loss	Notes/Results

Friday

Company	Opening Price	ATR	Volume	Entry Price	Target Price	Stop Loss	Notes/Results

Notes

FEBRUARY 2026

SUN	MON	TUE	WED	THU	FRI	SAT
1 Snow Moon	2	3	4	5	6	7
8	9	10	11	12	13	14
15	16 Presidents' Day Market Closed	17	18	19	20	21
22	23	24	25	26 Mercury Retrograde Begins ☿	27	28

February 2026 Trading Log Week 1

Monday

Company	Opening Price	ATR	Volume	Entry Price	Target Price	Stop Loss	Notes/Results

Tuesday

Company	Opening Price	ATR	Volume	Entry Price	Target Price	Stop Loss	Notes/Results

Wednesday

Company	Opening Price	ATR	Volume	Entry Price	Target Price	Stop Loss	Notes/Results

Thursday

Company	Opening Price	ATR	Volume	Entry Price	Target Price	Stop Loss	Notes/Results

Friday

Company	Opening Price	ATR	Volume	Entry Price	Target Price	Stop Loss	Notes/Results

February 2026 Trading Log Week 2

Monday

Company	Opening Price	ATR	Volume	Entry Price	Target Price	Stop Loss	Notes/Results

Tuesday

Company	Opening Price	ATR	Volume	Entry Price	Target Price	Stop Loss	Notes/Results

Wednesday

Company	Opening Price	ATR	Volume	Entry Price	Target Price	Stop Loss	Notes/Results

Thursday

Company	Opening Price	ATR	Volume	Entry Price	Target Price	Stop Loss	Notes/Results

Friday

Company	Opening Price	ATR	Volume	Entry Price	Target Price	Stop Loss	Notes/Results

February 2026 Trading Log Week 3

Monday

Company	Opening Price	ATR	Volume	Entry Price	Target Price	Stop Loss	Notes/Results

Tuesday

Company	Opening Price	ATR	Volume	Entry Price	Target Price	Stop Loss	Notes/Results

Wednesday

Company	Opening Price	ATR	Volume	Entry Price	Target Price	Stop Loss	Notes/Results

Thursday

Company	Opening Price	ATR	Volume	Entry Price	Target Price	Stop Loss	Notes/Results

Friday

Company	Opening Price	ATR	Volume	Entry Price	Target Price	Stop Loss	Notes/Results

February 2026 Trading Log Week 4

Monday

Company	Opening Price	ATR	Volume	Entry Price	Target Price	Stop Loss	Notes/Results

Tuesday

Company	Opening Price	ATR	Volume	Entry Price	Target Price	Stop Loss	Notes/Results

Wednesday

Company	Opening Price	ATR	Volume	Entry Price	Target Price	Stop Loss	Notes/Results

Thursday

Company	Opening Price	ATR	Volume	Entry Price	Target Price	Stop Loss	Notes/Results

Friday

Company	Opening Price	ATR	Volume	Entry Price	Target Price	Stop Loss	Notes/Results

Notes

MARCH 2026

SUN	MON	TUE	WED	THU	FRI	SAT
1	2	3 Worm Moon	4	5	6	7
8	9	10	11	12	13	14
15	16	17	18	19	20 Mercury Retrograde Ends	21
22	23	24	25	26	27	28
29	30	31				

March 2026 Trading Log Week 1

Monday

Company	Opening Price	ATR	Volume	Entry Price	Target Price	Stop Loss	Notes/Results

Tuesday

Company	Opening Price	ATR	Volume	Entry Price	Target Price	Stop Loss	Notes/Results

Wednesday

Company	Opening Price	ATR	Volume	Entry Price	Target Price	Stop Loss	Notes/Results

Thursday

Company	Opening Price	ATR	Volume	Entry Price	Target Price	Stop Loss	Notes/Results

Friday

Company	Opening Price	ATR	Volume	Entry Price	Target Price	Stop Loss	Notes/Results

March 2026 Trading Log Week 2

Monday

Company	Opening Price	ATR	Volume	Entry Price	Target Price	Stop Loss	Notes/Results

Tuesday

Company	Opening Price	ATR	Volume	Entry Price	Target Price	Stop Loss	Notes/Results

Wednesday

Company	Opening Price	ATR	Volume	Entry Price	Target Price	Stop Loss	Notes/Results

Thursday

Company	Opening Price	ATR	Volume	Entry Price	Target Price	Stop Loss	Notes/Results

Friday

Company	Opening Price	ATR	Volume	Entry Price	Target Price	Stop Loss	Notes/Results

March 2026 Trading Log Week 3

Monday

Company	Opening Price	ATR	Volume	Entry Price	Target Price	Stop Loss	Notes/Results

Tuesday

Company	Opening Price	ATR	Volume	Entry Price	Target Price	Stop Loss	Notes/Results

Wednesday

Company	Opening Price	ATR	Volume	Entry Price	Target Price	Stop Loss	Notes/Results

Thursday

Company	Opening Price	ATR	Volume	Entry Price	Target Price	Stop Loss	Notes/Results

Friday

Company	Opening Price	ATR	Volume	Entry Price	Target Price	Stop Loss	Notes/Results

March 2026 Trading Log Week 4

Monday

Company	Opening Price	ATR	Volume	Entry Price	Target Price	Stop Loss	Notes/Results

Tuesday

Company	Opening Price	ATR	Volume	Entry Price	Target Price	Stop Loss	Notes/Results

Wednesday

Company	Opening Price	ATR	Volume	Entry Price	Target Price	Stop Loss	Notes/Results

Thursday

Company	Opening Price	ATR	Volume	Entry Price	Target Price	Stop Loss	Notes/Results

Friday

Company	Opening Price	ATR	Volume	Entry Price	Target Price	Stop Loss	Notes/Results

Notes

APRIL 2026

SUN	MON	TUE	WED	THU	FRI	SAT
			1 Pink Moon	2	3 Good Friday Market Closed	4
5 Easter Sunday	6	7	8	9	10	11
12	13	14	15	16	17	18
19	20	21	22	23	24	25
26	27	28	29	30		

April 2026 Trading Log Week 1

Monday

Company	Opening Price	ATR	Volume	Entry Price	Target Price	Stop Loss	Notes/Results

Tuesday

Company	Opening Price	ATR	Volume	Entry Price	Target Price	Stop Loss	Notes/Results

Wednesday

Company	Opening Price	ATR	Volume	Entry Price	Target Price	Stop Loss	Notes/Results

Thursday

Company	Opening Price	ATR	Volume	Entry Price	Target Price	Stop Loss	Notes/Results

Friday

Company	Opening Price	ATR	Volume	Entry Price	Target Price	Stop Loss	Notes/Results

April 2026 Trading Log Week 2

Monday

Company	Opening Price	ATR	Volume	Entry Price	Target Price	Stop Loss	Notes/Results

Tuesday

Company	Opening Price	ATR	Volume	Entry Price	Target Price	Stop Loss	Notes/Results

Wednesday

Company	Opening Price	ATR	Volume	Entry Price	Target Price	Stop Loss	Notes/Results

Thursday

Company	Opening Price	ATR	Volume	Entry Price	Target Price	Stop Loss	Notes/Results

Friday

Company	Opening Price	ATR	Volume	Entry Price	Target Price	Stop Loss	Notes/Results

April 2026 Trading Log Week 3

Monday

Company	Opening Price	ATR	Volume	Entry Price	Target Price	Stop Loss	Notes/Results

Tuesday

Company	Opening Price	ATR	Volume	Entry Price	Target Price	Stop Loss	Notes/Results

Wednesday

Company	Opening Price	ATR	Volume	Entry Price	Target Price	Stop Loss	Notes/Results

Thursday

Company	Opening Price	ATR	Volume	Entry Price	Target Price	Stop Loss	Notes/Results

Friday

Company	Opening Price	ATR	Volume	Entry Price	Target Price	Stop Loss	Notes/Results

April 2026 Trading Log Week 4

Monday

Company	Opening Price	ATR	Volume	Entry Price	Target Price	Stop Loss	Notes/Results

Tuesday

Company	Opening Price	ATR	Volume	Entry Price	Target Price	Stop Loss	Notes/Results

Wednesday

Company	Opening Price	ATR	Volume	Entry Price	Target Price	Stop Loss	Notes/Results

Thursday

Company	Opening Price	ATR	Volume	Entry Price	Target Price	Stop Loss	Notes/Results

Friday

Company	Opening Price	ATR	Volume	Entry Price	Target Price	Stop Loss	Notes/Results

Notes

MAY 2026

SUN	MON	TUE	WED	THU	FRI	SAT
					1 Flower Moon	2
3	4	5	6	7	8	9
10	11	12	13	14	15	16
17	18	19	20	21	22	23
24	25 Memorial Day Market Closed	26	27	28	29	30
31 Blue Moon						

May 2026 Trading Log Week 1

Monday

Company	Opening Price	ATR	Volume	Entry Price	Target Price	Stop Loss	Notes/Results

Tuesday

Company	Opening Price	ATR	Volume	Entry Price	Target Price	Stop Loss	Notes/Results

Wednesday

Company	Opening Price	ATR	Volume	Entry Price	Target Price	Stop Loss	Notes/Results

Thursday

Company	Opening Price	ATR	Volume	Entry Price	Target Price	Stop Loss	Notes/Results

Friday

Company	Opening Price	ATR	Volume	Entry Price	Target Price	Stop Loss	Notes/Results

May 2026 Trading Log Week 2

Monday

Company	Opening Price	ATR	Volume	Entry Price	Target Price	Stop Loss	Notes/Results

Tuesday

Company	Opening Price	ATR	Volume	Entry Price	Target Price	Stop Loss	Notes/Results

Wednesday

Company	Opening Price	ATR	Volume	Entry Price	Target Price	Stop Loss	Notes/Results

Thursday

Company	Opening Price	ATR	Volume	Entry Price	Target Price	Stop Loss	Notes/Results

Friday

Company	Opening Price	ATR	Volume	Entry Price	Target Price	Stop Loss	Notes/Results

May 2026 Trading Log Week 3

Monday

Company	Opening Price	ATR	Volume	Entry Price	Target Price	Stop Loss	Notes/Results

Tuesday

Company	Opening Price	ATR	Volume	Entry Price	Target Price	Stop Loss	Notes/Results

Wednesday

Company	Opening Price	ATR	Volume	Entry Price	Target Price	Stop Loss	Notes/Results

Thursday

Company	Opening Price	ATR	Volume	Entry Price	Target Price	Stop Loss	Notes/Results

Friday

Company	Opening Price	ATR	Volume	Entry Price	Target Price	Stop Loss	Notes/Results

May 2026 Trading Log Week 4

Monday

Company	Opening Price	ATR	Volume	Entry Price	Target Price	Stop Loss	Notes/Results

Tuesday

Company	Opening Price	ATR	Volume	Entry Price	Target Price	Stop Loss	Notes/Results

Wednesday

Company	Opening Price	ATR	Volume	Entry Price	Target Price	Stop Loss	Notes/Results

Thursday

Company	Opening Price	ATR	Volume	Entry Price	Target Price	Stop Loss	Notes/Results

Friday

Company	Opening Price	ATR	Volume	Entry Price	Target Price	Stop Loss	Notes/Results

Notes

JUNE 2026

SUN	MON	TUE	WED	THU	FRI	SAT
	1	2	3	4	5	6
7	8	9	10	11	12	13
14	15	16	17	18	19 Juneteenth Market Closed	20
21	22	23	24	25	26	27
28	29 Mercury Retrograde Begins Strawberry Moon	30				

June 2026 Trading Log Week 1

Monday

Company	Opening Price	ATR	Volume	Entry Price	Target Price	Stop Loss	Notes/Results

Tuesday

Company	Opening Price	ATR	Volume	Entry Price	Target Price	Stop Loss	Notes/Results

Wednesday

Company	Opening Price	ATR	Volume	Entry Price	Target Price	Stop Loss	Notes/Results

Thursday

Company	Opening Price	ATR	Volume	Entry Price	Target Price	Stop Loss	Notes/Results

Friday

Company	Opening Price	ATR	Volume	Entry Price	Target Price	Stop Loss	Notes/Results

June 2026 Trading Log Week 2

Monday

Company	Opening Price	ATR	Volume	Entry Price	Target Price	Stop Loss	Notes/Results

Tuesday

Company	Opening Price	ATR	Volume	Entry Price	Target Price	Stop Loss	Notes/Results

Wednesday

Company	Opening Price	ATR	Volume	Entry Price	Target Price	Stop Loss	Notes/Results

Thursday

Company	Opening Price	ATR	Volume	Entry Price	Target Price	Stop Loss	Notes/Results

Friday

Company	Opening Price	ATR	Volume	Entry Price	Target Price	Stop Loss	Notes/Results

June 2026 Trading Log Week 3

Monday

Company	Opening Price	ATR	Volume	Entry Price	Target Price	Stop Loss	Notes/Results

Tuesday

Company	Opening Price	ATR	Volume	Entry Price	Target Price	Stop Loss	Notes/Results

Wednesday

Company	Opening Price	ATR	Volume	Entry Price	Target Price	Stop Loss	Notes/Results

Thursday

Company	Opening Price	ATR	Volume	Entry Price	Target Price	Stop Loss	Notes/Results

Friday

Company	Opening Price	ATR	Volume	Entry Price	Target Price	Stop Loss	Notes/Results

June 2026 Trading Log Week 4

Monday

Company	Opening Price	ATR	Volume	Entry Price	Target Price	Stop Loss	Notes/Results

Tuesday

Company	Opening Price	ATR	Volume	Entry Price	Target Price	Stop Loss	Notes/Results

Wednesday

Company	Opening Price	ATR	Volume	Entry Price	Target Price	Stop Loss	Notes/Results

Thursday

Company	Opening Price	ATR	Volume	Entry Price	Target Price	Stop Loss	Notes/Results

Friday

Company	Opening Price	ATR	Volume	Entry Price	Target Price	Stop Loss	Notes/Results

Notes

JULY 2026

SUN	MON	TUE	WED	THU	FRI	SAT
			1	2 Market Closes Early – 1 p.m.	3 Independence Day Holiday Market Closed	4 Independence Day
5	6	7	8	9	10	11
12	13	14	15	16	17 ♥	18
19	20	21	22	23 Mercury Retrograde Ends ☿	24	25
26	27	28	29 Buck Moon	30	31	

July 2026 Trading Log Week 1

Monday

Company	Opening Price	ATR	Volume	Entry Price	Target Price	Stop Loss	Notes/Results

Tuesday

Company	Opening Price	ATR	Volume	Entry Price	Target Price	Stop Loss	Notes/Results

Wednesday

Company	Opening Price	ATR	Volume	Entry Price	Target Price	Stop Loss	Notes/Results

Thursday

Company	Opening Price	ATR	Volume	Entry Price	Target Price	Stop Loss	Notes/Results

Friday

Company	Opening Price	ATR	Volume	Entry Price	Target Price	Stop Loss	Notes/Results

July 2026 Trading Log Week 2

Monday

Company	Opening Price	ATR	Volume	Entry Price	Target Price	Stop Loss	Notes/Results

Tuesday

Company	Opening Price	ATR	Volume	Entry Price	Target Price	Stop Loss	Notes/Results

Wednesday

Company	Opening Price	ATR	Volume	Entry Price	Target Price	Stop Loss	Notes/Results

Thursday

Company	Opening Price	ATR	Volume	Entry Price	Target Price	Stop Loss	Notes/Results

Friday

Company	Opening Price	ATR	Volume	Entry Price	Target Price	Stop Loss	Notes/Results

July 2026 Trading Log Week 3

Monday

Company	Opening Price	ATR	Volume	Entry Price	Target Price	Stop Loss	Notes/Results

Tuesday

Company	Opening Price	ATR	Volume	Entry Price	Target Price	Stop Loss	Notes/Results

Wednesday

Company	Opening Price	ATR	Volume	Entry Price	Target Price	Stop Loss	Notes/Results

Thursday

Company	Opening Price	ATR	Volume	Entry Price	Target Price	Stop Loss	Notes/Results

Friday

Company	Opening Price	ATR	Volume	Entry Price	Target Price	Stop Loss	Notes/Results

July 2026 Trading Log Week 4

Monday

Company	Opening Price	ATR	Volume	Entry Price	Target Price	Stop Loss	Notes/Results

Tuesday

Company	Opening Price	ATR	Volume	Entry Price	Target Price	Stop Loss	Notes/Results

Wednesday

Company	Opening Price	ATR	Volume	Entry Price	Target Price	Stop Loss	Notes/Results

Thursday

Company	Opening Price	ATR	Volume	Entry Price	Target Price	Stop Loss	Notes/Results

Friday

Company	Opening Price	ATR	Volume	Entry Price	Target Price	Stop Loss	Notes/Results

Notes

AUGUST 2026

SUN	MON	TUE	WED	THU	FRI	SAT
						1
2	3	4	5	6	7	8
9	10	11	12	13	14	15
16	17	18	19	20	21	22
23	24	25	26	27	28 Sturgeon Moon	29
30	31					

August 2026 Trading Log Week 1

Monday

Company	Opening Price	ATR	Volume	Entry Price	Target Price	Stop Loss	Notes/Results

Tuesday

Company	Opening Price	ATR	Volume	Entry Price	Target Price	Stop Loss	Notes/Results

Wednesday

Company	Opening Price	ATR	Volume	Entry Price	Target Price	Stop Loss	Notes/Results

Thursday

Company	Opening Price	ATR	Volume	Entry Price	Target Price	Stop Loss	Notes/Results

Friday

Company	Opening Price	ATR	Volume	Entry Price	Target Price	Stop Loss	Notes/Results

August 2026 Trading Log Week 2

Monday

Company	Opening Price	ATR	Volume	Entry Price	Target Price	Stop Loss	Notes/Results

Tuesday

Company	Opening Price	ATR	Volume	Entry Price	Target Price	Stop Loss	Notes/Results

Wednesday

Company	Opening Price	ATR	Volume	Entry Price	Target Price	Stop Loss	Notes/Results

Thursday

Company	Opening Price	ATR	Volume	Entry Price	Target Price	Stop Loss	Notes/Results

Friday

Company	Opening Price	ATR	Volume	Entry Price	Target Price	Stop Loss	Notes/Results

August 2026 Trading Log Week 3

Monday

Company	Opening Price	ATR	Volume	Entry Price	Target Price	Stop Loss	Notes/Results

Tuesday

Company	Opening Price	ATR	Volume	Entry Price	Target Price	Stop Loss	Notes/Results

Wednesday

Company	Opening Price	ATR	Volume	Entry Price	Target Price	Stop Loss	Notes/Results

Thursday

Company	Opening Price	ATR	Volume	Entry Price	Target Price	Stop Loss	Notes/Results

Friday

Company	Opening Price	ATR	Volume	Entry Price	Target Price	Stop Loss	Notes/Results

August 2026 Trading Log Week 4

Monday

Company	Opening Price	ATR	Volume	Entry Price	Target Price	Stop Loss	Notes/Results

Tuesday

Company	Opening Price	ATR	Volume	Entry Price	Target Price	Stop Loss	Notes/Results

Wednesday

Company	Opening Price	ATR	Volume	Entry Price	Target Price	Stop Loss	Notes/Results

Thursday

Company	Opening Price	ATR	Volume	Entry Price	Target Price	Stop Loss	Notes/Results

Friday

Company	Opening Price	ATR	Volume	Entry Price	Target Price	Stop Loss	Notes/Results

Notes

SEPTEMBER 2026

SUN	MON	TUE	WED	THU	FRI	SAT
		1	2	3	4	5
6	7 Labor Day	8	9	10	11	12
13	14	15	16	17	18	19
20	21	22	23	24	25	26 Harvest Moon
27	28	29	30			

September 2026 Trading Log Week 1

Monday

Company	Opening Price	ATR	Volume	Entry Price	Target Price	Stop Loss	Notes/Results

Tuesday

Company	Opening Price	ATR	Volume	Entry Price	Target Price	Stop Loss	Notes/Results

Wednesday

Company	Opening Price	ATR	Volume	Entry Price	Target Price	Stop Loss	Notes/Results

Thursday

Company	Opening Price	ATR	Volume	Entry Price	Target Price	Stop Loss	Notes/Results

Friday

Company	Opening Price	ATR	Volume	Entry Price	Target Price	Stop Loss	Notes/Results

September 2026 Trading Log Week 2

Monday

Company	Opening Price	ATR	Volume	Entry Price	Target Price	Stop Loss	Notes/Results

Tuesday

Company	Opening Price	ATR	Volume	Entry Price	Target Price	Stop Loss	Notes/Results

Wednesday

Company	Opening Price	ATR	Volume	Entry Price	Target Price	Stop Loss	Notes/Results

Thursday

Company	Opening Price	ATR	Volume	Entry Price	Target Price	Stop Loss	Notes/Results

Friday

Company	Opening Price	ATR	Volume	Entry Price	Target Price	Stop Loss	Notes/Results

September 2026 Trading Log Week 3

Monday

Company	Opening Price	ATR	Volume	Entry Price	Target Price	Stop Loss	Notes/Results

Tuesday

Company	Opening Price	ATR	Volume	Entry Price	Target Price	Stop Loss	Notes/Results

Wednesday

Company	Opening Price	ATR	Volume	Entry Price	Target Price	Stop Loss	Notes/Results

Thursday

Company	Opening Price	ATR	Volume	Entry Price	Target Price	Stop Loss	Notes/Results

Friday

Company	Opening Price	ATR	Volume	Entry Price	Target Price	Stop Loss	Notes/Results

September 2026 Trading Log Week 4

Monday

Company	Opening Price	ATR	Volume	Entry Price	Target Price	Stop Loss	Notes/Results

Tuesday

Company	Opening Price	ATR	Volume	Entry Price	Target Price	Stop Loss	Notes/Results

Wednesday

Company	Opening Price	ATR	Volume	Entry Price	Target Price	Stop Loss	Notes/Results

Thursday

Company	Opening Price	ATR	Volume	Entry Price	Target Price	Stop Loss	Notes/Results

Friday

Company	Opening Price	ATR	Volume	Entry Price	Target Price	Stop Loss	Notes/Results

Notes

OCTOBER 2026

SUN	MON	TUE	WED	THU	FRI	SAT
				1	2	3
4	5	6	7	8	9	10
11	12 Columbus Day	13	14	15	16	17
18	19	20	21	22	23	24 Mercury Retrograde Begins ☿
25	26 Hunter's Moon	27	28	29	30	31

October 2026 Trading Log Week 1

Monday

Company	Opening Price	ATR	Volume	Entry Price	Target Price	Stop Loss	Notes/Results

Tuesday

Company	Opening Price	ATR	Volume	Entry Price	Target Price	Stop Loss	Notes/Results

Wednesday

Company	Opening Price	ATR	Volume	Entry Price	Target Price	Stop Loss	Notes/Results

Thursday

Company	Opening Price	ATR	Volume	Entry Price	Target Price	Stop Loss	Notes/Results

Friday

Company	Opening Price	ATR	Volume	Entry Price	Target Price	Stop Loss	Notes/Results

October 2026 Trading Log Week 2

Monday

Company	Opening Price	ATR	Volume	Entry Price	Target Price	Stop Loss	Notes/Results

Tuesday

Company	Opening Price	ATR	Volume	Entry Price	Target Price	Stop Loss	Notes/Results

Wednesday

Company	Opening Price	ATR	Volume	Entry Price	Target Price	Stop Loss	Notes/Results

Thursday

Company	Opening Price	ATR	Volume	Entry Price	Target Price	Stop Loss	Notes/Results

Friday

Company	Opening Price	ATR	Volume	Entry Price	Target Price	Stop Loss	Notes/Results

October 2026 Trading Log Week 3

Monday

Company	Opening Price	ATR	Volume	Entry Price	Target Price	Stop Loss	Notes/Results

Tuesday

Company	Opening Price	ATR	Volume	Entry Price	Target Price	Stop Loss	Notes/Results

Wednesday

Company	Opening Price	ATR	Volume	Entry Price	Target Price	Stop Loss	Notes/Results

Thursday

Company	Opening Price	ATR	Volume	Entry Price	Target Price	Stop Loss	Notes/Results

Friday

Company	Opening Price	ATR	Volume	Entry Price	Target Price	Stop Loss	Notes/Results

October 2026 Trading Log Week 4

Monday

Company	Opening Price	ATR	Volume	Entry Price	Target Price	Stop Loss	Notes/Results

Tuesday

Company	Opening Price	ATR	Volume	Entry Price	Target Price	Stop Loss	Notes/Results

Wednesday

Company	Opening Price	ATR	Volume	Entry Price	Target Price	Stop Loss	Notes/Results

Thursday

Company	Opening Price	ATR	Volume	Entry Price	Target Price	Stop Loss	Notes/Results

Friday

Company	Opening Price	ATR	Volume	Entry Price	Target Price	Stop Loss	Notes/Results

Notes

NOVEMBER 2026

SUN	MON	TUE	WED	THU	FRI	SAT
1	2	3	4	5	6	7
8	9	10	11 Veterans Day	12	13 Mercury Retrograde Ends ☿	14
15	16	17	18	19	20	21
22	23	24 Beaver Moon	25	26 Thanksgiving Day Market Closed	27 Market Closes Early - 1 p.m.	28
29	30					

November 2026 Trading Log Week 1

Monday

Company	Opening Price	ATR	Volume	Entry Price	Target Price	Stop Loss	Notes/Results

Tuesday

Company	Opening Price	ATR	Volume	Entry Price	Target Price	Stop Loss	Notes/Results

Wednesday

Company	Opening Price	ATR	Volume	Entry Price	Target Price	Stop Loss	Notes/Results

Thursday

Company	Opening Price	ATR	Volume	Entry Price	Target Price	Stop Loss	Notes/Results

Friday

Company	Opening Price	ATR	Volume	Entry Price	Target Price	Stop Loss	Notes/Results

November 2026 Trading Log Week 2

Monday

Company	Opening Price	ATR	Volume	Entry Price	Target Price	Stop Loss	Notes/Results

Tuesday

Company	Opening Price	ATR	Volume	Entry Price	Target Price	Stop Loss	Notes/Results

Wednesday

Company	Opening Price	ATR	Volume	Entry Price	Target Price	Stop Loss	Notes/Results

Thursday

Company	Opening Price	ATR	Volume	Entry Price	Target Price	Stop Loss	Notes/Results

Friday

Company	Opening Price	ATR	Volume	Entry Price	Target Price	Stop Loss	Notes/Results

November 2026 Trading Log Week 3

Monday

Company	Opening Price	ATR	Volume	Entry Price	Target Price	Stop Loss	Notes/Results

Tuesday

Company	Opening Price	ATR	Volume	Entry Price	Target Price	Stop Loss	Notes/Results

Wednesday

Company	Opening Price	ATR	Volume	Entry Price	Target Price	Stop Loss	Notes/Results

Thursday

Company	Opening Price	ATR	Volume	Entry Price	Target Price	Stop Loss	Notes/Results

Friday

Company	Opening Price	ATR	Volume	Entry Price	Target Price	Stop Loss	Notes/Results

November 2026 Trading Log Week 4

Monday

Company	Opening Price	ATR	Volume	Entry Price	Target Price	Stop Loss	Notes/Results

Tuesday

Company	Opening Price	ATR	Volume	Entry Price	Target Price	Stop Loss	Notes/Results

Wednesday

Company	Opening Price	ATR	Volume	Entry Price	Target Price	Stop Loss	Notes/Results

Thursday

Company	Opening Price	ATR	Volume	Entry Price	Target Price	Stop Loss	Notes/Results

Friday

Company	Opening Price	ATR	Volume	Entry Price	Target Price	Stop Loss	Notes/Results

Notes

DECEMBER 2026

SUN	MON	TUE	WED	THU	FRI	SAT
		1	2	3	4	5
6	7	8	9	10	11	12
13	14	15	16	17	18	19
20	21	22	23 Cold Moon	24 Market Closes Early – 1 p.m.	25 Christmas Market Closed	26
27	28	29	30	31		

December 2026 Trading Log Week 1

Monday

Company	Opening Price	ATR	Volume	Entry Price	Target Price	Stop Loss	Notes/Results

Tuesday

Company	Opening Price	ATR	Volume	Entry Price	Target Price	Stop Loss	Notes/Results

Wednesday

Company	Opening Price	ATR	Volume	Entry Price	Target Price	Stop Loss	Notes/Results

Thursday

Company	Opening Price	ATR	Volume	Entry Price	Target Price	Stop Loss	Notes/Results

Friday

Company	Opening Price	ATR	Volume	Entry Price	Target Price	Stop Loss	Notes/Results

December 2026 Trading Log Week 2

Monday

Company	Opening Price	ATR	Volume	Entry Price	Target Price	Stop Loss	Notes/Results

Tuesday

Company	Opening Price	ATR	Volume	Entry Price	Target Price	Stop Loss	Notes/Results

Wednesday

Company	Opening Price	ATR	Volume	Entry Price	Target Price	Stop Loss	Notes/Results

Thursday

Company	Opening Price	ATR	Volume	Entry Price	Target Price	Stop Loss	Notes/Results

Friday

Company	Opening Price	ATR	Volume	Entry Price	Target Price	Stop Loss	Notes/Results

December 2026 Trading Log Week 3

Monday

Company	Opening Price	ATR	Volume	Entry Price	Target Price	Stop Loss	Notes/Results

Tuesday

Company	Opening Price	ATR	Volume	Entry Price	Target Price	Stop Loss	Notes/Results

Wednesday

Company	Opening Price	ATR	Volume	Entry Price	Target Price	Stop Loss	Notes/Results

Thursday

Company	Opening Price	ATR	Volume	Entry Price	Target Price	Stop Loss	Notes/Results

Friday

Company	Opening Price	ATR	Volume	Entry Price	Target Price	Stop Loss	Notes/Results

December 2026 Trading Log Week 4

Monday

Company	Opening Price	ATR	Volume	Entry Price	Target Price	Stop Loss	Notes/Results

Tuesday

Company	Opening Price	ATR	Volume	Entry Price	Target Price	Stop Loss	Notes/Results

Wednesday

Company	Opening Price	ATR	Volume	Entry Price	Target Price	Stop Loss	Notes/Results

Thursday

Company	Opening Price	ATR	Volume	Entry Price	Target Price	Stop Loss	Notes/Results

Friday

Company	Opening Price	ATR	Volume	Entry Price	Target Price	Stop Loss	Notes/Results

Notes

Section 2

Stock Market Investing Simplified

Investing in the stock market involves a strong commitment of time and money. There are many ways to invest, and each choice has its own set of rules and strategies. Choosing an investment method depends on your level of Risk Aversion or Risk Tolerance, and it also depends on how you answer these questions:

How much money can you invest without fear? How much time can you commit to company research and brokerage platform training or simulation practice? How quickly do you want to see your account grow? Will you trade with a cash or margin account? After considering these issues, you must choose a pathway for investing:

1. **Investing for dividends** – Invest in strong companies that may or may not offer fast growth, but will pay monthly, quarterly, or annual dividends. Look for high-quality companies with strong financial statements. Be prepared to reinvest dividends while holding these assets for long periods of time.

2. **Investing for growth** –Invest in innovative companies that can survive volatile markets. Look for high-quality companies with strong fundamentals. Expect to buy and hold these assets while remaining alert to quarterly earnings and other news.

3. **Investing for short-term gains** – Swing trading – look for seasonal patterns and target entry/exit levels for short-term investments. Accounts may expand exponentially over a few days, weeks or months. May also involve buying options to leverage funds.

4. **Investing for daily gains** - Pattern Day Trading (PDT) – Plan to enter and exit a trade on the same day; company fundamentals are less important because price momentum is the main issue. Look to enter and exit a trade in the shortest possible time frame, focusing full attention between 7 a.m. and 10 a.m. Must fully understand how to read candlestick signals and patterns.

Stock Market Resources for Company Research

Here is a brief list of useful resources for company research:

Company Websites

Yahoo Finance

CNBC

Tradingview.com

Finviz.com

Reddit

International Energy Agency

US Energy Information Administration

Federal Reserve Branches

AI Tools: ChatGPT, Meta AI, Grok, Gemini, and Perplexity

The checklist of resources above will help you make informed decisions before you invest in a company. Use the resource list to locate the information below before trading or investing in a company.

Company earnings, balance sheets, cash flow reports

Profit margins/PEG ratio, the P/E Multiple, and the "Rule of 40"

Debt, expenses, personnel turnover

Seasonality and past performance

CEO's vision and management's reputation

Product innovation and scale, industry forecasting

Consumer opinion

*Conference calls

** Locate recordings or transcripts of quarterly conference calls to gain insight from industry leaders such as: Apple, Microsoft, Nvidia, Netflix, Google, Meta, Walmart, Target, Home Depot, CrowdStrike, Proctor and Gamble, Starbucks, Pepsi, Eli Lilly, Merck, AT&T and others.*

Key Technical Analysis Terms

ATR – Average True Range is a technical analysis indicator that measures market volatility. ATR shows how much an asset typically moves, but not which direction. A stock with an ATR of $3.50 generally moves about $3.50 per day. A move of $1.00 is less volatile than a move of $5.00. The ATR is helpful when determining ranges for setting a target or stop loss.

EMA – Exponential Moving Average is a type of moving average used in technical analysis that gives more weight to recent prices. EMAs can be more responsive to price changes than the Simple Moving Average (SMA). EMAs can act like moving support or resistance levels. For instance, if a stock's 20-day EMA is rising and price stays above it, an upward trend is anticipated. When price falls below the EMA, a downtrend may be possible.

FIBS - Fibonacci levels help identify potential support and resistance levels based on the Fibonacci sequence. The most important level is the Golden Ratio, 0.618 (or 61.8%), which shows up in nature, geometry, and financial markets. Fibs will work best when combined with other indicators like moving averages or trendlines.

MACD - Moving Average Convergence Divergence is a momentum and trend-following indicator used in technical analysis to identify changes in the strength, direction, and duration of a trend. MACD helps avoid false signals that occur when using moving averages or momentum indicators alone. The tool works in all timeframes—intraday, daily, and weekly.

RSI - Relative Strength Index is a popular momentum oscillator in technical analysis that measures the speed and change of price movements. RSI tells you whether an asset is overbought or oversold, helping traders spot potential reversals or trend continuations. An RSI rating of 70 and above means "overbought," indicating price may be too high and a drop is possible. An RSI rating of 30 and below means "oversold," indicating the low price has the potential to rise. An RSI of 50 indicates a neutral zone. The RSI tool is best used with other indicators like MACD or trendlines.

VWAP - Volume Weighted Average Price is a trading benchmark that gives the average price of an asset, adjusted for volume, over a specific period. VWAP is usually calculated intraday, beginning at the market open. Institutions use VWAP to make large trades without drastically moving the market. VWAP acts as a dynamic line that price often respects. If price is above VWAP buyers are in control (bullish bias). If price is below VWAP, sellers are in control (bearish bias).

Sample Trading Plan

🕓 1. Prepare Before the Market Opens

Successful day trading starts *before* the bell rings.

Key Steps:

- **Review market news:** Check premarket movers, earnings reports, and major economic events (e.g., CPI data, Fed announcements).
- **Mark support and resistance levels:** Use premarket highs/lows or previous day's levels.
- **Plan your watchlist:** Choose 3–5 stocks with strong volume, volatility, and a clear catalyst.

🗝 *Goal:* Be focused. You can't trade everything — pick high-probability setups only.

🕓 2. Define Your Trading Plan

A written trading plan keeps you disciplined and consistent.

Include:

- Entry and exit rules (based on your setup, e.g., breakout, pullback)
- Stop-loss and target levels (define risk/reward)
- Maximum loss per trade (usually 1–2% of your account)
- Maximum total loss per day (e.g., 5%)

🗝 *Example:* If you risk $100 per trade with a 1:2 R:R, you'll make $200 if right, lose $100 if wrong.

🕓 3. Use Technical Analysis

Day traders rely heavily on charts and patterns.

Focus On:

- **Price action:** Candlestick formations, volume spikes, and trend strength.
- **Indicators (optional):** VWAP, moving averages (EMA 9/20), RSI, MACD.
- **Chart patterns:** Flags, pennants, breakouts, double bottoms, etc.

🗝 *Tip:* Keep it simple — too many indicators can cause confusion or hesitation.

---

4. Set Entry, Stop, and Target Before You Click Buy

Never enter without knowing your **risk-to-reward ratio** (R:R).

Example:

- **Entry:** $50
- **Stop-loss:** $49 (risk $1)
- **Target:** $52 (reward $2)
  → R:R = 1:2

This ensures **you only take trades that can make at least double what you risk.**

---

5. Manage Risk Aggressively

Capital preservation is your lifeline.

Rules:

- Risk **1–2% per trade**, never more.
- Use **stop-loss orders** (hard or mental).
- Avoid **revenge trading** after a loss.
- Know your **daily stop** (when to walk away).

Discipline beats excitement every time.

---

6. Use Proper Timing

Timing is critical for day trading.

Typical market rhythm:

- **First 30–60 minutes:** High volatility (good for experienced traders).
- **Midday (11am–2pm):** Slower, lower volume (scalpers stay cautious).
- **Final hour:** Renewed momentum (day's direction often becomes clear).

🕓 7. Journal Every Trade
A trade journal reveals your strengths and mistakes.

Include:
- Stock name, entry/exit, reason for entry, R:R ratio
- Screenshot of the chart
- Notes on emotion or hesitation

🗝 *Goal:* Find patterns in your winning and losing trades.

🕓 8. Control Your Emotions
Day trading is 80% psychology.

Learn to:
- Accept losses quickly.
- Avoid chasing moves.
- Stick to your plan even if you're wrong.

🗝 Remember: **Consistency > excitement.**

Example Routine Summary

Step	Task	Time
Pre-market	Review watchlist, mark key levels	8:00–9:30 AM
Market open	Trade your setups (risk-managed)	9:30–11:00 AM
Midday	Review trades, avoid overtrading	11:00 AM–2:00 PM
Close	Optional last trades, journal, recap	2:00–4:00 PM

Section 3

Company Watchlist

Company Name and Symbol	52-Week Hi/Lo	Earnings Date	PEG Ratio/P/E Multiple/ Rule of 40	Company News

Company Watchlist

Company Name and Symbol	52-Week Hi/Lo	Earnings Date	PEG Ratio/P/E Multiple/ Rule of 40	Company News

Company Watchlist

Company Name and Symbol	52-Week Hi/Lo	Earnings Date	PEG Ratio/P/E Multiple/ Rule of 40	Company News

Dividend Record

Company	Purchase Date	Type (M/Q/Y)	Yield %	#Shares	Amount	Pay Date

Dividend Record

Company	Purchase Date	Type (M/Q/Y)	Yield %	#Shares	Amount	Pay Date

Username and Password Log

Website or Account	Username	Password

Notes

Notes

Notes

Notes

Notes

Made in the USA
Monee, IL
11 November 2026

67971465R00057